SACRED MASCULINE

SACRED MASCULINE IS BOOK TWO OF THE NEW EDEN SERIES

OTHER BOOKS BY JAMES GALLUZZO

Sacred Feminine *(Book One of the New Eden Series)*
A Spiritual Handbook: A Resource for Travelers and Guides on the Journey
The Spirituality of Mary Magdalene
Jesus as Liberator and the Gospel Values
Quotes and Reflection Questions for Journaling your Spiritual Journey
Spiritual Writing: Be the Author of Your Own Story
Stop Whining, Choose Life.

SACRED MASCULINE

James Galluzzo

Gray Wings Press, LLC
Milwaukie, Oregon
2014

SACRED MASCULINE

By James Galluzzo

Library of Congress Control Number: 2014931165

Copyright © 2014 James Galluzzo

All rights are reserved under International and Pan-American Copyright Conventions.

No part of this book may be used or reproduced in any manner without permission except in the case of brief quotations in critical articles or reviews.

Requests should be forwarded to diversityasgift@comcast.net

or sent to Gray Wings Press, P.O. Box 593, Clackamas, OR 97015

ISBN 978-0615954813

Dedicated to
Charlie Kreiner
Joe Uveges
Bill Lynch
To the men of Breakthrough
To the men and women in my spiritual support group
who have supported my liberation
My men's group:
Bob Grover, Lyle Lindsey, David Lundstedt,
Terry Jones, Joe Bender and Scott Borrison

SACRED MASCULINE
Six Paintings

The Sacred Masculine has to be remembered and rediscovered just like the Sacred Feminine has to be brought out of exile. The Sacred Masculine has been buried in patriarchy and hierarchy and has lost its groundedness and its sacredness.

Because of culture, status, power, money and religion, men have been conditioned away from their authentic selves. Fear, ridicule, sexuality, loss of prestige or power have made it difficult for men to be liberated from the conditioned male image and role. Refusing this image is very challenging, but the result is the gift of being fully human.

As the old black and white poster in the sixties boldly said, "There will be no freedom until both women and men are free." As both men and women embrace the Sacred Masculine and Sacred Feminine, we will move to a world of peace, connectedness and wholeness.

By James Galluzzo

"WITHIN EVERY MOMENT THERE IS ONLY THE EMPTINESS
OF YIN RECEIVING THE FULLNESS OF YANG.
THIS IS THE ETERNAL MARRIAGE
OF MAN AND THE SACRED, OF HEAVEN AND EARTH."

MANTAK CHIA

INTRODUCTION

This book explains my six Sacred Masculine paintings. The inspiration began with a workshop on *Men and Masculinity* and from working with Charlie Kreiner, a central leader in the men's liberation movement. I created these paintings in 2013. I used watercolor, egg tempera, ink and markers on heavy watercolor paper. Then I added my own calligraphy over the artwork.

These paintings explore and embrace the Sacred Masculine. They are a visual example of key themes of the masculine journey—*father, king, warrior, lover, healer* and *grounded one*. They include the four basic archetypes and two themes that connect men to their call and to the earth, the universe and all that is holy.

Each chapter discusses one painting and its wording followed by a set of prayers and hymns that speak to the painting and explain its symbology.

THE SACRED MASCULINE FRAMEWORK

In the last twenty years, there has been an interest in the Sacred Masculine. I believe the reason for this is that men are beginning to connect to their spirituality. This has been a real challenge because for thousands of years culture and religion have framed gods in a male gender. Men are used to thinking of God as male, and blindly accept it as fact without questioning other images of the Sacred. It is through questioning and searching that men can bring together the sacred and the masculine, compassion with passion.

The framework of the male god comes from four directions.

1. THE MALE GODS

    The Greek and Roman mythical male gods of ancient times were primarily male heroes, manipulators, power- and control-seekers who fought among themselves. They include Zeus, Poseidon, Neptune, Kronos, Saturn, Pluto, Jupiter, Apollo, Hermes, Mercury, Hades, Mars and Ares. Whether it be the ancient gods of Greece and Rome, their names changed but not their roles.

2. THE MONOTHEISTIC GOD

    Jews and Christians rejected the multiple gods in favor of one god who was all-powerful (Monotheism).

3. THE ARCHETYPE/UNIVERSAL MODEL

    This model existed as part of the work of the men's movement through Robert Bly, Robert Moore, Houston Smith and others. The archetypes focus on the King, Warrior, Magician and Lover. There is the positive side and the shadow side for each model.

    The King: The good king looks out for the good of all people. He leads with respect and is fully conscious of healthy leadership. He focuses on order, law and direction. **The shadow king** rules with power and control and is intolerant of those who question his authority.

The Warrior: The good warrior fights for justice and works for peace. He is an activist filled with courage and thoughtfulness for the people and the earth. **The shadow warrior** is the bully, who enjoys violence and war for profit. The shadow warrior is often a coward and has low self-worth.

The Magician: The good magician is a healer and poet filled with vision, hope, possibilities and intuition. **The shadow magician** is the manipulator who uses his gifts to control and destroy.

The Lover: The good lover is sensual, compassionate, caring and loving to all people. He loves beauty, truth and connection. **The shadow lover** is needy, addictive and non-trusting. He lives in the Peter Pan mold and never wants to grow up because he can not accept responsibility or face the consequences of his actions.

These archetypes express the male figures of sacred spirituality. I have added the archetypes of **Father** and the **Grounded One** in my images to offer a fuller view of each man's personal journey.

4. RICHARD ROHR MODEL

Richard Rohr talks about the male spiritual journey in two stages.

The first stage is an ascent that deals with self-identity, discovery, sacrifice, self-control, potential power and sacrifice. Men set boundaries (what society tells them real men do) and move from boyhood to manhood. Men study, work, build a house and create families and do what they do well.

The second stage is a descent that starts somewhere between ages 35 and 50 years. Men search for wholeness and holiness. This involves questioning, letting go of old messages, taking risks, being humble, honesty and surrendering of control. This stage embraces connection and simplicity.

Some men never grow in the ascent stage because they want to be the wounded boy or desperate lover. Some men never grow in the descent stage because they refuse to look at where they are stuck, or because of their need to be perfect. They often believe the myth that men are fine just the way they are.

THE EMERGENCE OF THE SACRED MASCULINE
Why is rediscovering the Sacred Masculine so important?

I want to offer a different way of being human and a different way of being masculine. Men are being called to reach and embrace sacredness in their lives. This happens when men reclaim their humanity, respect who they are, live with integrity, see themselves as inherently good and honor the Sacred Feminine and spirituality within. This will allow for the Sacred Masculine to emerge.

Men need to stop believing in the old patriarchal and hierarchical models of "power over"—controlling and ruling the world and other human beings. The masculine model has been rigidly narrow for too long. It is clear men need a great deal of help, support and encouragement to effectively grow and evolve into their higher potential. Throughout history, the misaligned model of masculine power has been rooted also in judgment and steeped in control, domination and persecution in church matters, politics, the military and economics.

This model results in the selfish, self-serving misuse and abuse of "power over" less advantaged human beings and the resources of the earth. For many men, self-worth equals power, work, money and control leading to disconnection from others, the world, the earth and themselves.

To emerge, men will have to face the old message of what it means to be male, heal from pains and hurts, look at the unconscious part of themselves and face their demons. Then and only then, the Sacred Masculine will begin to restore honor, respect and integrity among men and women alike. Men do this, in part, by consciously calling the Sacred into themselves and seeing the Sacred in others.

Men must be honest in their thoughts and actions and live based on their inherent humanity. Men must choose the human model instead of living under the *shadow king,* the *wounded healer* or the *desperate lover.* Men must stop living out of fear, shame, never being enough and the "power over" model. They must learn to forgive themselves for buying into childhood messages—"don't cry," "don't be a sissy," "be tough," "be in control," "never show feelings," "don't be weak"—about what it means to be male. As men do this, they will embrace their humanity—connecting and relating to others, and their sacred divinity.

Chapter One: FATHER.................................... 1

Chapter Two: KING.................................... 7

Chapter Three: LOVER.................................... 13

Chapter Four: WARRIOR........................ 19

Chapter Five: HEALER................................ 25

Chapter Six: GROUNDED ONE........ 31

CHAPTER ONE:
FATHER

FATHER
(*as seen on painting*)

The Prodigal Father
Any Man can be a Father
Holding Family
Holy Father
My Precious One
Give my Lord a Try
Father's Day
Beloved Father
My Beloved Son
Our Father
Sacred Father
Father Sun
Father Time
Holding up the Son
Single Father
Dad
Son
Embracing the Wandering
Blessings by the Father

I added the **Father** archetype to the four traditional archetypes used to explain men. In this painting, I feel the father figure is so important to children, partners and a father's worldwide work. They can help the child grow in wisdom and knowledge. They are the first teachers and models along with their partners. They honor the precious one; they hold family together; they bless their children. From the ancient times of "Father Sun" to the modern idea that any man can be a father, "father" has been both a gift and a struggle for many men. This only works when the father is present to the child. It has been shown that the average American father spends only ten minutes of quality time with his child each day; that does not work.

When I taught in an all boys' high school, I challenged, encouraged and supported the young men to be all they could be. But I could only do so much. When they married and had children, the children taught them about caring, tenderness, patience, being present, and what unconditional love meant. A father might be reading the paper or looking at the stock market, and the child just crawls in his lap and expects to be loved.

When a father understands unconditional love, he can forgive, embrace and welcome his children home no matter what they did. He understands what it means to be a prodigal father.

The shadow father is manipulative, controlling, often abusive to those around him and never forgives.

Prayers to: FATHER

IN GRATITUDE FOR MY FATHER

I thank you for my father. He gave me the gift of life itself. He was such a good teacher and mentor, such a wonderful example of how to live a simple life so others can simply live. His messages of justice, peace, family, tradition, creativity, playfulness, culture and loyalty helped frame my life.

James Galluzzo

FOR A FATHER WHO HAS DIED

Father of Life, I thank you for my father. He was such a blessing to me while he was still with me. I still miss him so much. I thank you for what he left me as gifts of love and hope. I pray that he has enjoyed your embrace and that the relationship he and I have now might someday be renewed with you in heaven. I know that time is coming soon, I entrust him to your love and ask you to let him look out for me and to assist me to stay on the path to wholeness, diversity and love.

David Geraci

FOR FATHERS UNABLE TO EXPRESS LOVE AND AFFECTION

We pray for you, believing you did the best you could living in a society that ridiculed men for showing their feelings. You are not a victim or an oppressor. That might have been a role in the past but this is now. You are responsible for yourself. So as you grow in wisdom and knowledge, may you embrace your gifts of thinking, feeling, acting and deciding. May you be fully human and model for all young fathers who are trying to feel and love in a fuller way.

James Galluzzo

AS I PREPARE FOR MY WEDDING

Spirit of Life, these days are wonderful and filled with excitement as we prepare for my wedding. But in the rare quiet moments I sometimes see in my father's wonderful, familiar face, an uncertainty and a loss. He is such a good man and it is his role modeling that helped me choose a husband.

My father held my hand as I took my first steps. He will have my arm as we walk down the aisle on my wedding day. Bless him now as we each take steps toward new roles in life.

Help me to develop a newer, more adult relationship with my father, but one based on a lifetime of love and memories. Bless him and my mother and may they discover a greater freedom and depth in their love.

Creighton University Daily Reflections

FOR A FATHER CARRYING MANY BURDENS

Thank you, Father.

He is such a wonderful man and I love him with all my heart. Thank you for the gift he has been in my life.

Right now, he is struggling so much and has so many burdens to carry. I simply ask that you protect him from the pressures he is facing. If it is possible, relieve some of those pressures so that he can live with more peace and with so much less stress. Above all, I ask you to give him courage and hope. Let him keep it all in perspective and not lose his priorities. Let him have some fun and help him to stay close to those who love him and want to support him in all of this. Strengthen his faith in you so that he can be a living example of service, dedication, commitment and love to all the people with whom and for whom he works.

And, help me know how to support him and love him.

Your Son

Chapter Two:
KING

KING

(as seen on painting)

Earth King

Royal

A Good King Thinks Well of All People

Loyal

Kind

Honest

Justice

Rex

Thoughtful

Holy Grail

We Three Kings

Another

King of Kings

Boy King

Shadow King

Home

Loving King

Peacemaker

Lion King

I have a Dream

My Children

Joy, Peace, Love

Ruler

King of the Jews

Sky King

Star King

Moon King

The **King** painting captures the role of the good king. A good king looks out for the good of all people, loves beauty, listens, mediates, surrounds himself with creative people and invites the young and the old to give their ideas. He is loyal, brave, honest, thoughtful, and seeks peace and justice for all. The good king honors diversity and accepts all: women, men, children, the old, the young, gay and straight. He is relational, deeply committed to connection and has a special connection to the earth and to protecting the environment.

The shadow king is very self-centered. He is concerned with money, power and control. The shadow king isolates and is out of touch with the people. He surrounds himself with "yes" people, mainly older advisors, and does not like any questioning or creative thoughts that might challenge his way of thinking.

Prayers to: KING

May I achieve the perfect power of awakening.
Purifying the power of all contaminated actions.
Crushing the power of disturbing emotions at our root,
defusing the power of interfering forces;
I shall perfect the power of the Bodhisattva practice.
    (Buddhist Practice)

May I purify an ocean of worlds.
May I free an ocean of beings.
May I clearly see an ocean of Dharma.
May I realize an ocean of pristine wisdom.
May I purify an ocean of activities.
May I fulfill an ocean of aspirations.
May I make offerings to an ocean of Buddhas.
May I practice without discouragement for an ocean of eons.
To awaken fully through this Bodhisattva way,
I shall fulfill without exception all the diverse aspirations of the awakening practice of all Buddhas who journey to freedom.
    The Extraordinary Aspirations from the King of Prayers

O God of Israel, enthroned between the cherubim, you alone are God over all the kingdoms of the earth. You have made heaven and earth. Give ears and hear; open your eyes and see; listen to the words Sennacherib has sent to insult the living God.

2 Kings 19:15-17   (NIV)

Good king, we are in great need of your presence in our world. You look out for the good of all people. We are very divided and torn apart with liberal and conservative views, religious bigotry, fear, sexism, racism, homophobia and economic policies.

Please come to our assistance. Help us to respect one another, to show compassion and to practice loving kindness for and with all people. We do not have to all believe the same thing or live our lives the same way. But, please help us to live in harmony with one another, the earth and the universe.

James Galluzzo

Chapter Three
WARRIOR

WARRIOR
(as seen on painting)

Swords into Plowshares

Warrior God

Protector

Care

No Peace without Justice

World Peace

("Peace" in different languages)

Vede

Selam

Paz

Shalom

Pax

Peace

W R

A

PE CE

Power With

Prince of Peace

Fight for Justice

Dove

Warrior Chief

Bird of Peace

Fighting Evil

Lion and Lamb

Battle Cry

Warrior

The Warrior painting represents peace and justice. The warrior is the protector of the people. He fights evil, seeks justice for all and works tirelessly for peace. He is both the lion and the lamb. He works in the model of "power with" others rather than the model of "power over" others. No peace without justice is his mode of operation. As long as there is injustice there can be no peace.

His goal is to turn the swords into plowshares. He does this by not just fighting injustice but by breaking down unjust social structures.

The shadow warrior is about "power over," oppression, greed, violence and abuse.

Prayers to: WARRIOR

INVOCATION TO ST. MICHAEL

Dear St. Michael, the Archangel, protect our Warriors,
their bodies and souls, their followers and
anyone who would approach them with malicious intent.
Protect them, their bodies, and their hearts
as they travel about in their daily activities.
Protect them, their bodies, their homes, their property and
possessions from all retaliation.

St. Michael, intercede for these women and men with God
in all their necessities as your Warriors.
Mighty prince of the heavenly host and
victor over rebellious spirits, remember them in their weakness,
be for our Warriors, a powerful aid and, above all,
do not forsake them in our battles with the powers of evil. Amen.

NON-DENOMINATIONAL PRAYER

The Light of God surrounds those going into battle.
The Love of God enfolds them.
The Power of God protects them.
The Presence of God watches over them.
And, wherever they are, God is.

PRAYER OF ST FRANCIS

Make me an instrument of your peace,
Where there is hatred, let me sow love;
Where there is injury, pardon;
Where there is doubt, faith;
Where there is despair, hope;
Where there is darkness, light;
Where there is sadness, joy.

O Divine Master,
grant that I may not so much seek to be consoled,
as to console;
to be understood, as to understand;
to be loved, as to love.
For it is in giving that we receive.
It is in pardoning that we are pardoned,
and it is in dying that we are born to Eternal Life.
Amen.

They will beat our swords into plowshares and
our spears into pruning hooks.
Nation will not take up sword against nation,
nor will they train for war anymore.

Isaiah 2:4

Chapter Four
LOVER

LOVER
(as seen on painting)

Dreamers

Passion

Lovers

Brother, Sister

Heart Holder

To Be In Love

My Heart

Connected Always

Speak from the Heart

Smile

Man and Woman

Broken Heart

God and Goddess

Father and Son

Hands Across Anything

I Want to Hold Your Hand

Love Knows no Color

Relational

Partner

Friend

Strong

Tender

Kind

I Love You

A Full Heart

The **Lover** painting is filled with passion, connection, relationships and compassion. The lover sees all people as the beloved. He is strong, kind, gentle, passionate and loyal. He is a dreamer and speaks from the heart. The lover is often challenging for men because it is the great contradiction to old models of isolation, "power over" and self-interest.

Love is the essential ingredient for men to heal, to reconnect to others and themselves.

It is truly about embracing the Sacred Feminine that exists within and among every man. They cannot live fully if men have buried part of themselves. It is about merging the Sacred Masculine and Sacred Feminine. It is about embracing both within us and accepting the existence of the Sacred Feminine and allowing it to be expressed. It is about not settling for less.

The shadow lover is self-centered, controlling, and manipulative, doesn't trust anyone and sees no reason to change.

Prayers to: LOVER

A LOVER'S PRAYER

A life takes a heart
When the power of love comes together
Nothing can tear us apart
The touch of your hand I can feel
And it is stronger than steel

It's my silent message to you
Takes me there, my lover's prayer
And my soul is divided in two
When my love is on the line.

The mystery place blessed by us
And this truth is forever
In the face of incredible odds
And the look in your eyes tells me why
Let our story burn a sign in the sky.

Adapted from the Bee Gees

1979 BOOK OF COMMON PRAYER

O God, you have prepared for those who love you

such good things as surpass our understanding.

Pour into our hearts such love towards you, that we,

loving you in all things and above all things,

may obtain your promises, which exceed all that we can desire.

Amen.

I believe that lovers should be draped in flowers
And laid entwined together in a bed of clover,
Left there to sleep,
Left there to dream of happiness.

     Conor Oberst

Chapter Five
HEALER

HEALER
(as seen on painting)

Spirit One
Poet
Magician
Healing Spirit
Wellness
Magic
Heal
Healing Symbol
Poetry
Ink
Healing Arts
Healing Work
Peacemaker
Holy Man
Healing Stones
Healing Touch
Healing Water
Ying Yang
Lotus Flower
Healing Hand
Magic Tools
Safety
Magic Man

The **Healer** painting captures the role played by Merlin in the *Arthur* myth, by Jesus as a healer and by poets who bring a way of looking at the ying and yang. The healer offers comfort, tenderness, empathy, compassion and a healing hand. Healers, in all kinds of traditions, are holy men and women who are peacemakers, magicians, poets, artists and spirit-filled people. In the Native American tradition they are revered as medicine men and women.

The lotus flower is the great symbol of the Eastern healer. The healer uses healing arts *(creative practices)*, healing work *(energy activities)*, healing water and touch.

The shadow side of the healer is the trickster *(the deceiver or liar)* and manipulator.

PRAYERS TO: HEALER

THE HEALER'S PRAYER

Connect me to the universe, the mind of God.

Connect me to compassion, the heart of God.

Connect me to the earth, the manifested garden of God.

Connect me to infinity, the realm of God.

Connect me to others, the image of God.

Connect me that I represent the greatest good,
    the presence of God.

I connect to the flow of creation embracing the will of God.

Jerry Willis

There is so much good I can do for the planet.
At times, I may work for causes.
At other times, I may use
the power of my thoughts to help heal the planet.
If I hear news of a world disaster or
acts of senseless violence,
I immediately surround the whole situation with love.
I send positive energy and do visualizations, seeing the incident
working out with a solution that is best for everyone.

  Louise L. Hay

Let the Divine's love flow through me
and bring healing like a river,
cool and refreshing.
Both a stream of hope
and a torrent
washing away what needs to be gone.
Let it pour into my heart
And heal me.

  James Galluzzo

CHAPTER 6
GROUNDED ONE

GROUNDED ONE

(as seen on painting)

Fire Nation
World
Earth
Mountain Man
Bending Body Earth
Harvester
Discover
Farmer
Explorer
Father Earth
One
Timber
Birth
Protector of Peace
Handle with Care
Earth Kingdom
Rooted
Grounded One
Water, Earth, Fire, Air
Tend the Soil of the Earth
Deliver Food
Planter
Water Tribe
Man on the Planet
Father Sky
Animals
Mountains
Trees
Caring for Future Generations
Man on the Moon
Universe
Earthman
Keeping the Green
Planets
Stars
Tender
Love
Passion

The **Grounded One** painting is the most important addition to this series. Men are seen as being in their heads and connected to father sky as opposed to mother earth. But until men get grounded in the first chakra (the first of seven chakras, the one that grounds people to the earth, that connects them with nature, which means rooted in the earth) they cannot heal and cannot grow. Men must be rooted in the earth kingdom, must see their body in the earth and their deep connection to the earth. They have to walk in nature, plant a garden, cook dinner, tend the beauty around them, be good stewards of the animals, forests, rivers and earth's resources. The grounded one must care for future generations, keeping the gifts alive.

The Grounded One has to embrace father earth and be at one with the water, fire, air and earth. There can no longer be the dualistic thinking of mother earth and father sky. I hold that it can be mother and father sky and father and mother earth.

Being grounded is seeing all as brothers and sisters, as one, seeing our deep connection to all of creation and our relationship to the smallest cell and the greatest galaxy.

The shadow side of the grounded one is disconnection, staying in the head and isolation. He is not willing to ground himself rooted in the earth. Without the grounding, men often miss the space for questioning, for exploring, for thinking in new ways that prevents them from developing the spiritual journey.

PRAYERS TO:
GROUNDED ONE

Grounded One, keep me connected to others,
the earth, the universe and myself.
Help me to stay out of my head,
help me to be grounded in the first chakra and
help me to stay present
to my heart, soul, mind and body
so I can stay present to all
that is before me.

    James Galluzzo

May all I say and all I think be in harmony with thee,
God within me, God beyond me, maker of the trees.

    The Poetry of Sumer

Lord, the air smells good today
straight from the mysteries within the garden of God.
The trees in our prayer, the birds in praise,
the first blue violets, kneeling.

    Rumi

ISRAELI SUKOS SONG

Its harvest time. It's harvest time.

How rich is nature's yield

in fruit of earth and bush and tree,

from orchard, farm and field.

It's autumn time. It's autumn time.

When leaves turn gold and red.

In smiling sky and land and sea

God's glories are outspread.

It's Sukos time. It's Sukos time.

This day of our Thanksgiving.

We hymn the praise of God

above for all the joys of living.

This book emerges from my hope that all people understand the struggles and possibilities for men who commit to their spiritual journey. Then there will become a greater possibility for the Sacred Feminine and the Sacred Masculine to merge and create a connection to wholeness that will allow all people to live in peace, work together, bring about justice for all and honor to all living creatures, the earth, the universe, the cosmos and the sacred within and among us.

The gift of the sacred masculine energy is the embrace of the sacred human. The sacred human (the merger of the Sacred Masculine and Sacred Feminine, that is, being fully human) finds connection, relationships, equality and power. The result is joining the sacred and the human. The sacred human is how people connect to others, how they love, how they heal and how they show compassion. Joined together the Sacred Masculine and Sacred Feminine become love. The joining of the female and male, of two truths, allows all people to live in the mystery. In the mystery, the not knowing, humans can truly begin to love others and themselves. Love is the binder for the Sacred Masculine and Sacred Feminine, to be together with each person and among all people.

The third book in this series will merge the Sacred Masculine and Sacred Feminine as one.

"WISDOM IS THE SACRED COMMUNION OF THE MASCULINE AND FEMININE."

Victor Hugo

JAMES GALLUZO

JAMES GALLUZZO has been a spiritual director and guide for 25 years, working with individuals, teaching classes, and giving retreats. He is an artist, author, priest, teacher, administrator, diversity trainer, and spiritual director.

Fr. Galluzzo is the author of: The Sacred Feminine, A Spiritual Handbook: A Resource for Travelers and Guides on the Journey, The Spirituality of Mary Magdalene, Jesus as Liberator and the Gospel Values, Quotes and Reflection Questions for Journaling your Spiritual Journey, Spiritual Writing: Be the Author of Your Own Story, and Stop Whining, Choose Life.

He founded Allies: People to People, an organization that teaches a way of living and thinking that honors human liberation based on the Gospel values, and that works to end oppression of any kind: sexism, racism, classism, ageism, adultism, and homophobia.

Fr. Galluzzo is the director of the non-profit organization Diversity as Gift that works to honor all and teach about dignity from a spiritual perspective. He is also the director of the Urban Spirituality Center in Portland, Oregon.

He holds a BA degree from Gonzaga University, an MAT degree from Reed College, an Administrative Certificate from Lewis and Clark College, an MA degree in Theology from Catholic University of America, Mount Angel Seminary, and Portland State University.

Fr. Galluzzo leads workshops throughout the country on Conflict Resolution, Community Building, Diversity, Gospel Values, Spirituality, and Human Liberation.

ACKNOWLEDGEMENTS

Special thanks to:
Ann Faricy
Janet Beard
Sue Hammond
Maureen Schwerdtfeger
Bob Grover
Gerry Grover
Annie Doyle

Book and Cover Design by Karen Gatens, Gatens Design

www.ingramcontent.com/pod-product-compliance
Lightning Source LLC
Chambersburg PA
CBHW042003150426
43194CB00002B/113